Of all the classroom tools,
We're the smallest in the bunch,
But we're also the most beat up,
Damaged, bent, and crunched.

We sit atop the pencils,
Waiting to be kindly used,
But instead we end up broken,
Frequently being abused.

Sometimes they like to chew on us,
Or bite off a big chunk.
They don't treat us like the important tools we are.
Instead, we are treated like junk.

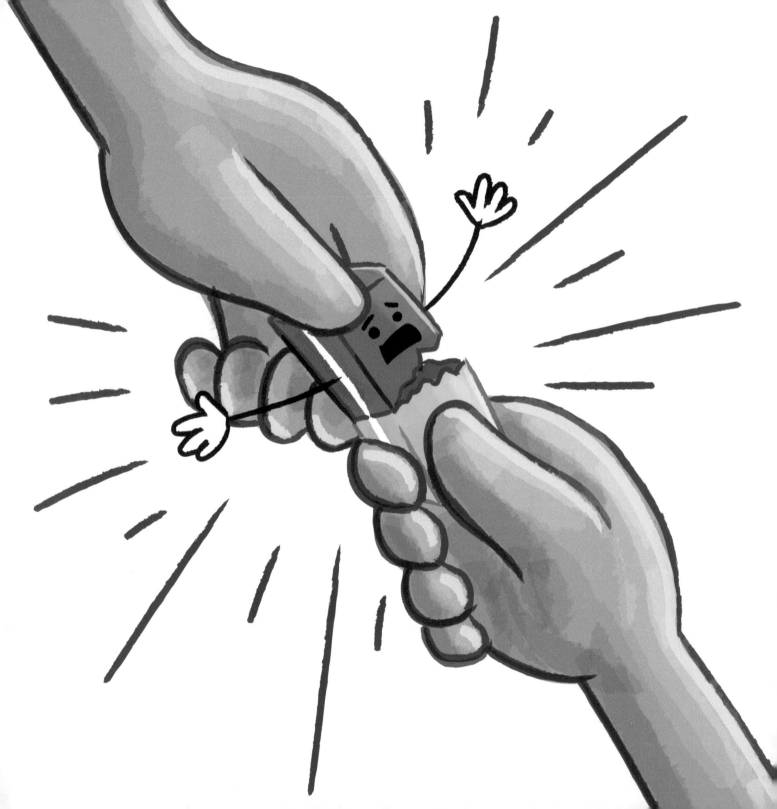

They rip us all apart,
And crumble us at their desks.
They don't care that they are rough with us,
Or that they make a mess.

Erasers of all kinds,
From the animal-shaped to large pink,
Started making our way to the cubbies
Right past the classroom sink.

We hid away in the cubbies
When they were outside for recess.
Hopefully, if they realized their lack of respect,
Our mission would be a success.

We asked the pencils to help us
Leave the children a simple note.
We would be gone when they got back.
And here is what we wrote:

We're tired of being mistreated,
So we're doing something you won't like.
You kids, you won't see us anymore –
Us erasers, we're going on strike!

Don't bother trying to find us
Until you've learned respect.
That's right, we are gone now!
The class erasers have LEFT!

The kids got back from lunch.
They didn't notice we were gone at first.
Then one student made an error,
And his eyes looked as if they would burst.

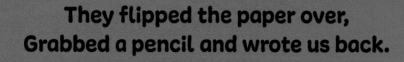

The students each took turns saying sorry,
And we erased their small mistakes.
Once they treated us correctly
Everything was great!

So be careful when you're in class,
That you treat your tools with care
Because you never know
They can go on strike and no longer be there!

Printed in the USA
CPSIA information can be obtained
at www.ICGtesting.com
LVHW061104290923
757852LV00009B/77